**This book is dedicated to
Entertainment Tonight**

They trained me to do clearance and without them I would not
have had a career.
Thanks so much!

I0487832

CLEARANCE SECRETS

TABLE OF CONTENTS

CLEARANCE SECRETS
A QUICK AND EASY GUIDE FOR THE BEGINNING AND
ADVANCED SCREENWRITER, DIRECTOR OR PRODUCER

CHAPTER ONE

MAKING A FILM

This book is intended for anyone who wants to make a movie or a biography or a documentary or a webisode.

Let me just say this is a workbook, not a legal tome. It will be written very simply from soup to nuts and if you are more experienced and see things you already know, then skip over them to something you didn't know.

It will cover the basics for making a simple feature film. It will also cover what the issues are for making a film with clips in it, be it a biograph, documentary etc.

So let's start with a simple feature film or TV show.

FEATURE FILM

Okay, so you and a friend of yours have come up with a great idea for a film. You sat down and hammered out the plot and the characters, found a screenplay program such as Final Draft or Movie Magic Screenwriting, and sweated and strained and finally have that first draft.

Did you spell check it? Those programs both have spell checks.
Or maybe it's too soon. Maybe a rewrite or two.

So now you have a shooting script. But before you hire a
director, actors, a cinematographer, there are other things to be
considered. I know. You're in a hurry to get going, but this is a
short book which you can carry with you and refer to when you
have questions.

THE SCRIPT

If you have a written a script, it belongs to you. If you have
written it with a friend or partner, then it belongs to both of you.
Or does it?

Unfortunately, there are immediately legal issues that crop up.

First of all, you need have an agreement in writing between the
two of you as to whether the profits (and expenses perhaps) will
be shared between you two equally. Or you can hire someone to
write the screenplay and set it up as a work for hire, in which you
pay the writer for his work up front and then you keep all the
profits.

If you hire a composer, then you also need an agreement for his
services and what that entails. You will also need agreements for
your cinematographer, your actors, and any other personnel
working on the film.

These sorts of agreements may be found in Appendix A of this
book.

COPYRIGHT

You have a copyright in your script or film once it is fixed in a
tangible medium of expression, which means that once you have
written it, filmed it, audiotaped it, etc.

But what happens if someone steals your work. Many people register it with the Writers Guild, which is about $30 and lasts for 5 years. But what does it really do for you? Nothing. It proves that you wrote it. There is also the really old suggestion of mailing it to yourself and not opening it and you have the postmark to prove when you wrote it.

But back to what happens if someone steals your work? The Writers Guild won't help you and neither will the envelope you mailed yourself. You could hire an expensive lawyer but the first thing she will say is "did you copyright this?"

This is because the US Copyright Law provides very strong punishment for stealing, such as up to and beyond $250,000. Registering your script with the Copyright Office will protect you. Don't put this off because you figure you will worry about it later. Later will come and you will have forgotten about. You can always register it if you change the title. Also you cannot get a distribution deal without Errors & Omissions insurance and they will want you to have your copyright registered. But more about that later.

SIMILARITY OF TITLES

What if your title is the same as someone else's...like "The Time Machine?" There are more than 15 listings for this title in IMDB (or the Internet Movie Database). What then?

You cannot copyright titles, only the expression of the title. Therefore, if your plot is completely different from the plot of the other films with the same title, there will not be a problem. However, it is always better to have a unique title because otherwise there may be a possibility of confusion between your film and others with the same title. Furthermore, there are certain films that are so famous that you cannot use their titles again. For example, use of a title which is indelibly linked in the public mind with a film or television program and has thus attained "secondary meaning" (such as "Gone With the Wind," for example) can subject you to litigation based upon the likelihood of confusion if the title is trademarked, or on passing off if it appears your title may be linked to some previous very successful film or book.

Also keep in mind that many times after the film is finished, the distributor will want to replace your title with something he/she likes better. So be prepared not to fall in love with your original title.

COPYRIGHT REGISTRATION

You may put off registering your copyright because it sounds confusing and difficult. It used to be but not anymore. All you have to do is go to www.copyrightoffice.gov. You will find a section that says Register a Copyright. Click on it and follow the instructions. For a screenplay, it is a literary work. Just fill in the information and pay the $35/$50 fee with a credit card and upload your script in pdf format to the website. They will confirm you have registered it and send you an email. They will send you a receipt andmake sure to hold on to the receipt because your registration will not show up in the Copyright Office for 6 to 8 months. So when you go to obtain Errors & Omissions insurance, you can just provide your receipt, which will be sufficient for them.

So you have copyrighted your screenplay, but when it is a finished film, you will also need to copyright the film. You follow the same procedure except you have send in a DVD of your film.

All right, all right, you're tired of all of the rules. You can certainly copyright your title later. You will have to eventually to get insurance to shoot your film, but many filmmakers don't do that until later. Let's move on.

So now you're ready to shoot. You've hired your actors (maybe just friends) and your cinematographer and maybe a production assistant or two. PLEASE BE SURE TO GET THEM TO SIGN AGREEMENTS BEFORE YOU START SHOOTING. In case you haven't noticed, best friends can become enemies in the blink of an eye. These agreements are also in Appendix A. Please use them.

5

CHAPTER TWO

COPYRIGHT LENGTH AND PUBLIC DOMAIN

Copyright lasts up to 70 years from the death of the author. Many people think that public domain, in which the copyright holder no longer needs to be contacted or compensated for the use of her work, is 100 years. It is 70 years plus the life of the author in the US because Senator Sonny Bono in 1990 changed it from the previous term. See below for more information on this subject.

LITERARY WORKS

Literary works, which include books, films, television programs, webisodes, art works, and still photos among other things, must be licensed from their owners. This is because the Copyright Act gives creators of literary works the right to sell or license these works and to make money from them for the period of the copyright.

NEW LENGTH OF COPYRIGHT

The Sonny Bono Copyright Term Extension Act of 1998, is the law that added 20 years to the duration of copyright. As a result of the Act, copyrights to pre-1978 works that would have lasted 75 years from their first publication now last 95 years; and copyrights to 1978 and more recent works whose copyrights would have lasted for the lives of their authors plus 50 years now last for the lives of their authors plus 70 years. This law was partially created in response to the length of copyright laws in foreign countries which have always been anywhere from 70 years plus the life of the author to 90 years from publication date. It is different in each country.

Once the copyright runs out, the creative work falls into the public domain and can be used freely by anyone without payment or licensing. If the work is not public domain, it is considered literary property, just like an automobile is property, and permission must be obtained from the owner for use of the material. The Copyright Act provides substantial penalties for copyright infringement ranging from $10,000 for accidental infringement to $250,000 for willful infringement.

There are websites that list public domain music such as pdinfo.com or Wikipedia that can be very helpful.

CHAPTER THREE

SCRIPT CLEARANCE

SHOOTING THE FILM

Before you shoot your film, you need to obtain a script clearance report. This is to avoid making huge mistakes and being unable to release your film because there are many things in the film that permission has to be obtained for their usage. There was a feature film created by an actor that he got into the Sundance Film Festival and it was received brilliantly. It was the opening for him as an actor, screenwriter and filmmaker. However, when a studio purchased it, they had to spend more than a million dollars to obtain permission for all the props, etc., that he used without permission. He's lucky that the distributor was no enamored of the film that he went ahead with the film. You don't want that to happen to you. It certainly doesn't have to happen to you especially if you follow the guidelines in this book. Also some things have changed with regarding clearance of trademarks (meaning using Jif Peanut Butter or Cheetos). That will be discussed later in this book.

WHAT A SCRIPT CLEARANCE REPORT CAN DO FOR YOU –

It can save your ass. And it should be done BEFORE you shoot the film.

NAME CLEARANCES

I'll bet you didn't know that you can't use a name without their being 3 people in the state in which your script takes place or in the whole United States if your film takes place "Anywhere USA. This is because some person may decide they don't like the way their name is used or because their name is used for a bad guy. Name clearance is important to avoid litigation. It is important to search a name in Los Angeles or New York if the film takes place there. If it is a generic USA, then we search nationwide. It is difficult to search names in foreign countries as many of them do not have name databases.

PROPS

Many props require clearance such as cereal boxes etc. and particularly these days, computers and cell phones and websites. Apple and Samsung phones must be cleared with Apple and Samsung or you could be subject to a lawsuit. Phone companies may give you permission for use of these phones if you use them according to their rules. You can't be shooting someone with a gun with an Iphone in the other hand. Apple will not allow it. The solution to this is to cover the logo and make sure the screen (which is also an Apple trademark) not be visible.

This is also true of COMPUTERS, COMPUTER SCREENS, and WEBSITES such as Facebook, Google, Instagram, Youtube and Vimeo among others.

HOWEVER, there is new thinking in the minds of many attorneys (which may not apply to certain film companies). If a trademark is used in the manner it was intended, is an incidental use (not focused on) or not derogatory, no clearance is required. This is especially true, if the products are only used in the background in a group such as in a grocery store

LOCATIONS

Many low budget filmmakers like to find a location, shoot and run. This is a bad idea. It is much better to get permission to shoot in a supermarket for instance. Usually, a location release can be free although occasionally the location may charge money. However, if you are shooting in someone's home, they will probably not have a problem signing a location release. See Appendix B for a location release form. There is another issue with this. Suppose you are shooting in Canada and pretend it is the US and want to use Shakey's Pizza Parlor signage. Sometimes, you can get permission but in this case, they did not have the authority to grant permission nationwide. When in doubt, create new names and have Clearance check them.

EDITING

Your film is shot and is in the can (these days it might be digital and there will be no can as there was when people shot on 35 mm film).

You and a friend decide to edit the film. You purchase an editing program such as IMovie which comes included in your Mac computer, Apple Final Cut Pro or Premiere Pro. If you don't have a Mac, Premiere has a program for non-Mac users as well as Pinnacle and Movavi Video. If you are experienced and good at learning, you will be rapidly editing your film.

This is the time for you to search for a distributor. If you get one or even if not, you will want to obtain a Copyright & Title Search to determine how many other films have the same title and may be in conflict with your own. Even if your film has an extremely unique title, the Errors & Insurance companies will generally require one as well as a script clearance report (based on your final shooting script) to issue insurance for your production. (see Chapter 11 for more info on Errors & Omissions insurance.

Cost for E&O insurance is approximately $3500 to $5000 for a $500,000 production for 3 years.

CHAPTER 4

USE OF PHOTOS

So you want to use still photos in your film or documentary.

STILL PHOTOS

Still photos fall into several categories.

PUBLICITY PHOTOS

Star headshots have in the past not been copyrighted and, since they have been disseminated to the public, they are generally considered public domain and therefore there is no necessity to clear them with the studio that produced them (if you can even determine who did). However, currently, because of the rule that you have a copyright as soon as you fix something in a tangible medium of expression, pretty much everything is copyrighted.

Consequently, clearance must be obtained from the photographer and sometimes the studio, since in the past, photographers photos were shot as work for hire and consequently belonged to the studios who hired them.

What about production stills?

PRODUCTION STILLS

Photos taken on the set of the film or TV show during the shooting) must be cleared with the studio and can cost anywhere between $150 and $500.

LOBBY CARDS (film posters)

These used to be lumped into the same category as publicity photos and did not require clearance unless they have a copyright notice on them. Currently, all lobby cards are copyrighted and must be cleared. Some like the old one for "The Maltese Falcon" were shot from footage not used in the film, so this one is public domain. But you would have to do a lot of research to determine this sort of thing. Best to clear them.

Okay, so you've seen a bunch of photos taken on the street or the red carpet. No, they're not public domain. They are owned by photographers who will come after you if you don't clear them.

PAPARAZZI PHOTOS

These have been taken by photographers such as Ron Galella) must be cleared with the photographer. If you don't, the photographer will show up and demand much more money than he would have charged had you gone to him in the first place. He might even sue you. Fees go from $500 to over $2000 for very famous photographers.

MAGAZINE COVERS

MAGAZINE COVERS AND BOOK COVERS involve two clearances:

1) the magazine

2) the photographer who took the photo.

This applies particularly to such magazines as Vanity Fair (you must also obtain permission from Annie Liebowitz), People (Steve Schapiro shoots a lot of their photos), Cosmopolitan (Francesco Scavullo) as well as Life and Playboy. Producers in the past have not cleared magazines such as Time and TV Guide, but now it is important to clear them. The caveat is if you are using a bunch of covers and not focusing on any of them, you may have a fair use exception (see discussion of fair use later).

It is easy, but not cheap, to license all sorts of generic photos as well as some famous photos.

STILL PHOTOS HOUSES

There are also photo houses such as Everett, Alamy, Shutterstock, AP Wide World Photo, Corbis, and Getty which will license photos to you which they have the right to do. The cost of licensing each photo varies from approximately $100 to $500 and up.

ART CREATED BY FRIENDS AND FAMILY

Permission and a release must be obtained even from your Mom if you she painted the painting on the wall in the living room where you are shooting. This means signed paperwork. If she didn't create it, you need to determine who did and obtain permission from the artist.

BEWARE OF

material that exists on location. Artwork, paintings, etc. must be cleared with their owners.

PHOTOS OF CAST MEMBERS

Permission is required from any photo/artwork subject who is not a cast member. If they are a cast member, make sure that permission to use their image is included in their talent agreement. Again, signed paperwork.

CHAPTER FIVE

USE OF CLIPS

HOME MOVIES

These photos are copyrighted and permission for their usage must be obtained. It is even more important in these situations for clearance to be obtained because these movies are private. Use of them impinges on the owner's right privacy as well as right of publicity. Consequently, use of them without permission will obtain greater punishment than use of photos created for general usage.

PUBLIC DOMAIN FILMS AND STILLS

Copyright term is now 70 years plus the life of the author. A work of art obtains a copyright as an unpublished work as soon as it is "fixed in a tangible medium of expression." If that work of art was not registered for copyright or does not have a notice of copyright on it and it is then "published" (which is accomplished by distribution to the public), it loses its unpublished copyright status and falls into the public domain. Once it is in the public domain, it can be reused by anyone without fear of copyright infringement since the copyright no longer exists.

However, the fact that a television program may not have a visible copyright notice on it does not indicate that it is public domain, since it could have been registered with the Library of Congress. The only way to determine whether a film or television show is copyrighted is to do a copyright search at the Library of Congress. This applies to all works prior to 1988. You can search the Copyright Office online back to 1978. Prior to that, you will have to hire a researcher at the Copyright Office to go there and go through their catalogs to determine the copyright status of any item.

Since 1988 when the U.S. joined the Berne Copyright Convention which states that no formalities are required to obtain a copyright and therefore no copyright notice is required nor is registration with the Library of Congress required. A program is copyrighted whether or not it has a copyright notice or is registered with the Library of Congress. However, most copyright holders still register their works with the Library of Congress and put copyright notices on them since there are benefits to them in lawsuits that arise out of the Copyright Act itself.

How about news footage?

NEWS AND/OR STOCK FOOTAGE

News organizations can license the footage that they have shot at press conferences to other entities. However, they can only license the copyright. They cannot license rights to the appearances of people who appear in the clips, including the anchor people, the news reporters and ordinary people who are interviewed on the show nor can they license any music used in the background of the clips. Use of these people's names and likenesses as well as the music usually requires additional clearances (discussed further below).

You have wasn't to use films or TV shows or news footage as playback on a TV show in your film.

FILM CLIPS

Any excerpt from a feature film must be licensed from the copyright holder, and an agreement negotiated for payment for use of the clips. Most studios charge a fee on the basis of a minute or fraction thereof. Most of them also will not license footage on an aggregate basis; i.e., adding all the seconds of a film used together to make up a minute. Usually, the studios charge on a per clip or per cut, per minute basis.

The cost per clip depends on the rights required. It is more expensive to license all rights in all media, worldwide in perpetuity than it is to license 5 years worldwide distribution in CD-Rom, for instance, even assuming that a studio will grant you perpetuity. It is less expensive to license all rights in all media worldwide in perpetuity excluding theatrical rights, when you are doing a documentary that will never air in a theatre.

Many studios are currently have their own interactive and multimedia divisions and therefore refuse to license material for other multimedia projects. Some studios have reciprocal arrangements with other studios and provide clips at a much lower fee on that basis. If your project is affiliated with a studio, it is important to determine up front if that studio has reciprocal deals in place which might apply to your project.

Most studios do not function in the same fashion as stock footage houses, who will frequently give you a lower rate if you license more material. The studios generally have an attitude that they are not a stock footage house and carefully monitor who is using their footage and how it is being used. If you are using the footage in a pejorative fashion, the studios will not license it to you. Occasionally, certain studios will give you a price break if you want to use 5 or more of their films. On the other hand, if you need too many of their films, they may decide they want a piece of your project.

Contrary to popular belief, there is no rule that says you can use 5 seconds for free. That 5 seconds will cost the same $10,000 as 1 minute. Therefore, it behooves you to use the entire scene you have licensed, rather than using 2-second clips from 6 scenes. Sometimes these days they will license material to you on a cumulative basis of more than one clip from a film or TV show, so it never hurts to ask.

The studio contracts also read that you may not edit the scenes, but this does not seem to apply in real life in that most programs cut from an interview to a clip, back to the interview and then back to the clip again, which is editing but the studios generally turn a blind eye to such things.

The studios do not care whether you license their footage or not, although these days some studios have quotas they need to fill and are more willing to license their material. They do not need your money. Furthermore, the agreements that they send you to sign are generally not negotiable and are very stringent, demanding all sorts of concessions from end credits to a guarantee that you will clear all the talent and the music used in the clip as well as an agreement that you will indemnify them against any claim that may arise as a result of the broadcast of the clip.

If you want the clip, you are going to have to sign their license, which is usually a "quitclaim" that not only will not warrant that the studio even owns the footage but rather than indemnifying you, requires that you indemnify the studio against liabilities that arise from the use of the footage. In a way, this is understandable since by broadcasting the material, you may be subjecting the studio to claims from third parties.

ADVERTISING AND PROMOTION

Studios rarely grant permission to use clips in advertising and promotion even when the producer offers substantial fees for this use. However, on occasion, you can beg them and they may grant it for an additional fee.

TELEVISION CLIPS

Television clips are owned by studios, independent production companies and TV networks and are handled in the same fashion as described above with regard to film clips.

Currently, all licensors are very concerned about usage of their material in "interactive" projects, by which they mean projects in which the images can be manipulated and changed so that they are no longer recognizable. They do not want to allow this to happen, so the word "interactive" in any letter requesting permission can elicit an immediate "no" unless you find a way to explain that you are simply able to view the material without changing it. Use of material in an interactive fashion will require serious negotiations.

CHAPTER SIX

USE OF PUBLIC FIGURES

So maybe you are working on a film about historical figures. Or you want to use public or private people in your film.

RIGHT OF PRIVACY

Under U.S. law, an individual has a right of privacy and his image cannot be used by another until he either consents to that use and thereby waives this right or until he becomes a public figure, either by placing himself in the limelight and making himself a person of public interest (such as becoming an actor or politician) or by some act which gives him a news significance (such as a serial killer like Jeffrey Dahmer whose actions are chronicled in the news media). Because they are public figures, consent is not required from public figures such as President Clinton and Marilyn Monroe when they appear in news footage, which includes material shot at a news conference covered by more than one news camera or celebrities arriving at an event such as the Academy Awards, etc., for which they were not contracted but appeared in public voluntarily.

This is because these public figures were aware that by appearing at the press conference they were giving permission for use of their appearances in the footage anywhere it might appear. This situation also applies to newsreels (such as Universal Newsreel) which ran in movie theatres in the forties and fifties and are very obviously news.

Suppose you want to use news commentators or anchors in your project.

PUBLIC FIGURES IN NEWS TELEVISION PROGRAMS

(interviewers-interviewees) - Public figures, such as Mike Wallace, Barbara Walters, etc., who appear in news programs must be cleared because these programs were produced under a union (SAG or AFTRA) contract. The union contracts require current consent and a negotiated payment for use of the appearance of any artist prior to the use of an excerpt from these programs in another program.

Consequently, anyone who appeared on a news/interview program such as "Person to Person," including the host, Edward R. Murrow, must be cleared because his or her appearance would constitute a performance under the union agreements. The fact that the program was produced under the auspices of the news wing of a network does not mean that the performer need not be cleared. It is important to differentiate between news and performance. Frequently, NBC News or other news organizations will clear these people for you and charge you for their appearances.

DECEASED PERSONS AND THE RIGHT OF PUBLICITY

A deceased person has no right of privacy in **New York** and many other states. **In California**, an estate may still have a right of publicity under the California Civil Code 3341. There is no post-humous right of publicity in New York and many other states. This right is triggered only when a person's image is used to sell or endorse products in print ads and commercials and does not apply to feature films or television programs, since they tell a story or disseminate information and do not sell a product and are considered artistic usages. Music videos are a borderline situation because they are created as tools to sell records and are occasionally considered to be musical commercials. However, the unions frequently require consent to be obtained from estates for use of deceased persons' likenesses in film clips in works such as multimedia projects, television programs, etc.

CHAPTER SEVEN

TALENT IN FEATURE FILMS AND TELEVISION

ACTORS

The Screen Actors Guild merged with AFTRA to become SAG/AFTRA. The Screen Actors Guild agreement specifies than when a producer desires to use an excerpt from a feature film, that producer must obtain current consent from all members of SAG (including actors, helicopter and airplane pilots and estates of deceased performers but excluding stunt performers) for use of the excerpt and negotiate a fee that can be no less than the current scale payment (see Appendix C for rates). Stars may waive this scale payment if they choose. Extras do not have to be cleared.

SAG/AFTRA provides that if you make a scale payment to the actor, there are no residuals for the reuse unless you want to use them in another program. Then they must be cleared and paid.

Check with SAG/AFTRA for current rates as they differ between projects created on film and those on videotape.

STUNTMEN

Beware of stuntmen. Because you can't see them and consequently cannot immediately determine how many of them need to be paid, the use of a clip can be very expensive. Until very recently, you used to have to obtain permission and negotiate a fee with each stunt person just as you do with SAG actors. Recently, the code was changed. Now all that is required is to obtain their payment information and send them a SAG scale payment. However, it is difficult to determine how many stunt people are in a scene, since frequently stunt credits are negotiated and not all the people who worked on the stunt are listed. The best approach is to assume that anything that vaguely looks like a stunt is one. The easiest way to determine the names of the stunt people is to contact the stunt coordinator and have him identify the stuntmen in the scene you are interested in. This is not always foolproof, since the stuntmen change from day to day and the coordinator is a busy man whose main interest is not your show. However, they are usually very cooperative, since they know that this means money to them and their friends.

PRE-1960 THEATRICAL FEATURE FILMS

Because prior to 1960, the SAG agreement did not contain any provision to pay residuals to actors appearing in feature film., Rule of thumb in the industry was that actors in these films did not require clearance or payment for use in clips. This was confirmed via a lawsuit between Screen Actors Guild and Universal and Disney. Now that SAG has merged with AFTRA, this also applied to pre-1960 AFTRA clips.

SAG WAIVERS

Permission not to clear and pay actors is very difficult to convince SAG/AFTRA to grant. Usually, they are only granted when there is a special reason, for example, profits of the show are going to charity. Usually, SAG will only permit you to ask stars to waive and to pay the non-stars a scale payment. They will still require current consent.

AGENT'S FEES

Agents are not allowed to take a commission on a scale payment. Therefore, when you are contacting an agent to obtain permission to use his client in a clip at scale, it is wise to offer a 10% commission. This ensures that the agent will pay attention to your request. Otherwise, he will put it under the three million dollar deals he has pending and you will never get an answer.

TELEVISION PROGRAMS

ACTORS

SAG and AFTRA are now one union, SAG/AFTRA. See previous notes regarding SAG/AFRA payments.

AFTRA

This is the union governing tape programs such as soap operas and variety shows. Many other tape programs, such as situation comedies, are governed by the SAG rules listed above. AFTRA also governs kinescopes, which were filmed version of early live and taped programs.

RATES

Although the unions are combined, AFTRA's payment schedules are more complicated than SAG's in that there is a separate scale payment for a half-hour show, an hour show, a 90-minute show, etc. There are also specialty act rates, under 5 lines and special business. Dancers and singers also must be cleared and paid. You don't even have to be able to see a dancer's face, just the body. Once again, extras do not need clearance or payment. However, determining who is an extra can be tricky because it does not depend on whether they speak, but how they were hired on the show. Worst case cost for AFTRA comes in the supplemental market area where they usually require that you approach them for a waiver, since supplemental markets are not addressed in the AFTRA agreement. The waiver can specify payment to each performer of double-scale for television shows and single scale for videocassette. Many times, in practice, producers do not obtain waivers and simply pay single scale to all performers. These are considerations to be decided on a case-by-case basis.

AFTRA has an advantage over SAG - there are no treble damages penalties. On the other hand, you must obtain a waiver from AFTRA to ask stars to waive. Each rerun of a show with AFTRA performers in it requires an additional payment, with the second run at 75% on down.

Check with the SAG/AFTRA website for current rates.

CHAPTER EIGHT

DIRECTORS AND WRITERS

Oh, you didn't know you had to pay the writers and directors of clips that you want to use. Wrong.

DIRECTORS AND WRITERS PAYMENTS

RATES

The Directors Guild and the Writers Guild have schedules of payments required each time clips are used in a multimedia program, film or television show. There are separate schedules for feature films and television programs, which apply to the origination of the clip, i.e., the fee is dependent on whether the clip came from a feature film or a television show. Feature films rates break at a 30-second rate while television rates are much more expensive, changing rates at a 10-second cutoff. Rates can be obtained from the guilds. (Rates are listed in Appendix C)

WAIVERS

They DO NOT give waivers except for the Oscars and the Emmys and for "a lecture about drug abuse at the PTA.".

ONE-TIME ONLY

However, the good news is that the payments are one-time only. There is no second payment when the show reruns or is distributed on home video.

SCHEDULES

A producer is required to keep track of the film or television programs writers and directors and the amount of time used and must submit the information with a check to the appropriate guild. Episode titles are required for television shows by the Writers Guild. The guilds then write their own checks to their members. DGA charges a 12.5% P&W on top of the clip fee while WGA does not charge P&W. Rates are dependent on the length of the clips and whether they are SAG or AFTRA programs.

COMPILATION RATE

If a producer is producing a program which is an anniversary show or the "Best of..," the DGA and WGA will levy a "compilation rate," which is a penalty for using all clips and not creating new material. This is based on whether the show is more than 75% clips, meaning that the 25% of the show is non-union clips and interviews.

This is because all of the unions would rather that a producer hire live talent rather than use clips. The compilation rate is dreaded, since it is much more than the per clip use rate would be. There are also several versions depending on the union: the daytime rate, the primetime rate, the variety rate. The rate is arrived at by multiplying the standard writer rate times 250% times the number of half hours in the program. Even if you pay a compilation rate, you must keep track of all clips used, their length and the writers and directors, so that the union can divide up the payment you make among the various writers/directors. The only time you would benefit from the compilation rate is when you are using many short television clips. If your program is comprised of many different elements, then a clip rate is much more economical.

Check with the DGA and WGA for current excerpt rates.

CHAPTER NINE

MUSIC CLEARANCE

When you use music, you have to obtain clearance unless you hire a composer and use his music. You still need a release from him, which should include payment. An agreement is composed of offer, acceptance and compensation. Compensation can be gratis, so your agreement should say "For valuable consideration, the receipt of which is hereby accepted."

SYNC LICENSES

Musical compositions are copyrighted just as films and television programs are and must be licensed for use. A song is composed of the words and music, which is also described as publishing. If a producer simply wants to have a character sing "Happy Birthday," he must obtain a synchronization license for use of the music publishing (to synchronize sound with picture) for this use. The fee varies depending on length of music used, how it is used (visual vocal, background instrumental, etc.), number of uses, media in which it is used to be used etc. Once again, it is prohibitively expensive to obtain all rights in all media for a composition, in the range starting usually $20,000. However, "Happy Birthday" is a bad example because a recent lawsuit has determined that "Happy Birthday" is in the public domain and no clearance is required.

QUOTES

Music is different from clips in that publishers will give a producer a quote for the use he is requesting. That quote will be good for 30 to 90 days, after which it may be withdrawn. Once a producer decides he wants to use the song and orders the license, he must then pay for the song. Publishers do not like to do all the work and then have it canceled at the last moment. Many times, a publisher will refuse to send off a request for a quote before the producer will agree they have the money for this. My recent responses for music clearance are $20,000 for publishing and

$20,000 for master clearance for a feature documentary or a feature film. Beware.

If a producer is unsure what rights he wants, it is wise to obtain a quote for the shortest usage requested and request options for all other uses. Option usually must be exercised within 12 to 24 months. This can save a producer a great deal of money, since if the program doesn't sell, he is not locked into a huge amount of money. With regard to CD-ROM and home video, publishers will generally negotiate a penny rate per tape sold with an advance against a certain number of units. You can ask for film festivals for 1 year and an option for 1 year, US only, basic cable and an option for worldwide use. You have to exercise these options within one (1) year usually, but it makes it possible to take your film to film festivals without it cost an astronomical sum.

MASTER LICENSES

If instead of having your character sing "Happy Birthday," a producer wants to use the Beatles version, he must license the master recording ("record"). Currently, "Happy Birthday" is in the public domain. However, if Journey records it, you must obtain permission for use of this recording. This necessitates contacting the record company which produced the version the producer wants to use and obtaining a quote for the use. The prices are at least the same, and many times much more than the sync prices. Many times, it is much more financially sensible to hire a musician with a studio and re-record the song, rather than use the original recording.

NEEDLEDROPS

A master license is required when a producer does a needledrop; i.e., uses a portion of a record under film footage, stills or another portion of his program without using the physical footage.

MUSIC IN FEATURE FILM AND TELEVISION PROGRAMS

Sometimes, when you purchase a clip which has music in it, the master comes with the clip, since the music was already fixed to the clip itself. Usually, this is not true such as when a record is used in a film and licensed for that film, and then a producer wants to use an excerpt. In that instance, the film's license will not transfer and the producer will have to obtain an additional license. Many film studios require that you obtain a master license in addition to the clip copyright license.

MUSICIANS UNION

Most feature films and most television programs use musicians who belong to the American Federation of Musicians (for example an orchestra or even a band). This union requires payment when the music is reused as a part of a film clip or a record. The AF of M is a murky area. No one seems to understand exactly how to relate to them. There are two agreements: the Film agreement and the TV agreement. Depending on which one your project falls under, the price is different. The TV agreement is much more expensive. CD-Rom and other new media has yet been addressed by this guild to my knowledge.

DEALS

Normally, there are several ways to make a deal with the AF of M. One is to pay $300 per musician per clip, so this can be expensive if you have lots of clips which all contain orchestras. If you have a problem of this sort, they suggest you submit the material to them and try to come to an arrangement. They are generally very helpful in giving you prices that fit your budget. But be warned, prices start about $20,000 per program. Recently, I worked with them and they gave me a price that was way too high ($20,000.) When I told them that, they went to another portion of their agreement and came back with a fee that was reasonable ($5000).

RECORDINGS

Use of a master recording is supposed to generate an AF of M payment. In practice, television producers rarely pay additional payment for use of records. This will also probably be true for multimedia usages. This is changing, however, and the AF of M is taking an active stance in pursuing payments.

CHAPTER 10

FAIR USE

Under the original Copyright Act, a creator of a work is entitled to be the only one who can grant permission for the use of his work. However, in order to avoid the creator having a monopoly on his work, the Copyright Act granted term limits to the use of created material after a certain period of time. This created works that fell into the public domain, meaning anyone can use them. Under the Copyright Act (revised in 1976), a creator has a common law copyright once the work has been fixed in a tangible medium of expression, meaning that he wrote it down or recorded it. However, unless the work is registered with the Copyright Office, this law and the monetary penalties it provides will not help you if you want to sue for copyright infringement.

The Copyright Act also provided another help to creators of new works: fair use. Under Section of 107 of the Copyright Act (which applies to all works one might want to create) states:

The fair use of a copyrighted work for purposes such as criticism, comment, news reporting teaching (including multiple copies for classroom use), scholarship, or research, is not an infringement of copyright. However, the Act left it up to the courts to decide whether such usage in an individual situation would be a fair use.

There are 4 factors that the courts take into consideration in determining whether a usage falls into fair use:

1.   The purpose and character of the use, including whether such use is of commercial nature or is for

        nonprofit educational purposes.

2.   The nature of the copyrighted work.

3.   The amount and substantial of the portion used in relation to the copyrighted work as a whole (did they use

        a lot of it or only a little, a de minimus usage).

4.   The effect of the use on the potential market for or value of the copyrighted work (publishing the most important part of a book prior to its promoted publication date, for example).

In short, a fair use boils down to the reason you are using it, what kind of work the copyrighted work is, how much was used and whether this eliminated the possibility of the copyright holder being able to make money off it. The most egregious example of a non-fair use is the time that a TV network took the entire film about a sports star created by an 18-year-old student and used it in a sports project of theirs without compensating the student or asking his peremission, which then eliminated the market in which the student could to sell his film.

Avoid trying to use fair use for advertising purposes, since the work is not being used in the manner it was intended and is being used for commercial purposes.

There are two (2) fair use cases that can explain more about how this works.
1) *Harper & Row v. Nation Enterprises*, 471 U.S. 539 (1985), was a United States Supreme Court decision in which public interest in learning about a historical figure's impressions of a historic event was held not to be sufficient to show fair use of material otherwise protected by copyright. Defendant, *The Nation*, had summarized and quoted substantially from *A Time to Heal*, president Gerald Ford's forthcoming memoir of his decision to pardon former president Richard Nixon. When Harper & Row, who held the rights to *A Time to Heal*, brought suit, *The Nation* asserted that its use of the book was protected under the doctrine of fair use, because of the great public interest in a historical figure's account of a historic incident. The Court rejected this argument holding that the right of first publication was important enough to find in favor of Harper. **The amount and substantiality of the portion used in relation to the copyrighted work as a whole weighed against a finding of fair use. Although the "amount" was small, it constituted a "substantial" portion of the work because the excerpt was the "heart**

of the work". The Court noted that an infringer could not defend plagiarism by pointing to how much else they could have plagiarized but did not.

2) Iowa State University Research Foundation, Inc., an Iowa corporation, Plaintiff-appellee, v. American Broadcasting Companies, Inc., a New York Corporation, an ABC Sports, Inc., a New York Corporation, Defendants-appellants, 621 F.2d 57 (2d Cir. 1980), During the 1970-71 college term, James Doran and another student enrolled at Iowa State University, supervised by Professor Richard Kraemer, produced a 28-minute film titled Champion. It presented a short biography of a fellow student, Dan Gable, a champion wrestler who was destined to win a gold medal at the 1972 Munich Olympics. The film was financed jointly by appellee Iowa State University Research Foundation ("Iowa") and the Gable family, and chronicled Gable's quest for excellence in wrestling. Throughout the film, comments by Gable, his family, coaches, and teammates accompanied footage of wrestling matches, training sessions, and Gable's home life. Iowa obtained a valid statutory copyright and retained all rights to Champion, except that it granted Doran the right to license its first television showing, but only with "the full knowledge and consent of the University." Doran proceeded to attempt, without success, to sell the television rights to a number of potential customers, including ABC, the National Broadcasting Co., and the Hughes Sports Network. Thus, prior to the summer of 1972, the film was rented exclusively to high school wrestling coaches, service organizations, and sports booster clubs. **Although ABC thus admitted virtually all allegations of copying, it raised the defense of fair use. Following a two-day bench trial on the issue of liability in September 1978, Judge Lumbard rejected the defense, finding that no agreement had ever been reached by Doran and ABC. Indeed, he noted, Iowa had not been consulted prior to the network's telecasts of portions of Champion and was therefore unable to "consent" to ABC's use as required**

by its own agreement with Doran. Accordingly, the judge found that "defendants appropriated something of value for which, from the nature and extent of their business, they were well prepared to pay," rendering their use of Champion "unfair.

It is better to consult a fair use attorney before you decide whether to fair use a clip, which avoids the possibility of a lawsuit.

PARODY AND SATIRE

PARODY

Parody is another situation in which fair use is acceptable. The caveat is that the parody must comment directly on a copyrighted work that is the subject of the parody. The factors are that it must be a new, copyrightable work, based on a previously copyrighted work, recognizable as the previous work but not taking more from that work than is necessary, criticizes or comments on the subject matter of the copyrighted work and will not affect the market for the previous work. One example of what is not parody is the book that was all ready to be published by Simon & Schuster entitled "The Cat Not in the Hat," which used the Dr. Seuss format but was not commenting on the Dr. Seuss book but on the O.J. Simpson trial. The publishers lost and never published the book, based mostly on how much of the Dr. Seuss book was used.

1) Campbell v. Acuff-Rose Music, Inc., 510 U.S. 569 (1994), was a United States Supreme Court copyright law case **that established that a commercial** parody **can qualify as** fair use. This case established that the fact that money is made by a work does not make it impossible for fair use to apply; it is merely one of the components of a fair use analysis.

SATIRE

Satire comments on some aspect of society and, as such, is frequently acceptable as a fair use. This tends to apply to comedy shows and editorial uses.

CHAPTER 11

USE OF VIDEO FROM WIKIPEDIA AND OTHER ONLINE SOURCES

CREATIVE COMMONS LICENSES

Today many works can be found on the internet that can be used under a Creative Commons license. There are four kinds of licenses, three of which you don't want to use. Read the titles. If they say "non-commercial" or "no derivatives," stay away from them because they will forbid your ability to sell your project. There are two others, "Attribution-Share Alike 4.0 International" and "Attribution 4.0 International." Only use the fourth one. The Share-Alike one says that you will let others use your creation on the same basis that you are obtaining their license. You will not be able to get any film distributor or book publisher will want to work with you if you permit others to use your work on this basis. This one also says you need to identify the source and spell out that it is being used pursuant to this Creative Commons license. The big problem is that it contains a provision that says that your work cannot have copyright protection put on it by the distributors to protect the work. There are penalties for breaking these copyright protection locks.

Other attorneys have done additional research on the Wikimedia Creative Commons licenses and discovered that most studios and many distributors (including Disney and NBC) will not accept these licenses because they say you may not use a digital rights management system or DRM on your work with this license. DRMs are the digital locks that distributor put on DVDs so that no one can copy them. Under a new law passed in the 1990s called the Digital Millennium Copyright Act (DMCA), it is a crime to break digital locks even to copy public domain material that would be on a locked DVD. Using a Creative Commons license could be an impediment to your getting a DVD or Blu-Ray deal. We suggest you not use any Creative Commons licenses.

There are other places to obtain photos including the National Archives and stock photo and footage houses without these issues.

MPAA TITLE REGISTRATION – DO NOT JOIN

The Motion Picture Association of America founded the MPAA Title Registration system to avoid litigation over identical or similar film titles intended for use in the U.S. An independent filmmaker should not join this organization for several reasons. First of all, joining means you agree to an arbitration with arbitrators culled from major motion picture companies who may be biased based on economic issues which are weighted in favor of the studio. Studios who have joined this group have been required to change their titles even when it doesn't appear that the titles are going to be an issue. For example, the Weinstein Company was forced to change its title "The Butler," to "Lee Daniel's The Butler," because Warner Bros. insisted that its name infringed on a now-lost 1916 silent short film of the same name. However, since it only applies to its members, there are forty-seven (47) listings for the title "Butler" in the U.S. Copyright Office.

CHAPTER 12

ERRORS AND OMISSIONS INSURANCE

In order to obtain distribution for your film, you will need to obtain Errors & Omissions insurance (see previous info re cost).

Many insurance companies require the following reports in order to give you a quote and the insurance.

SCRIPT CLEARANCE REPORTS

A Script Clearance Report is frequently requested by Errors and Omissions insurance companies to minimize the possibility of legal claims. Such a report will alert the producer to areas of possible legal exposure in the script by checking all names and noting conflicts with actual or otherwise protected names or entities. It also checks not only names of characters, but also businesses, schools, organizations, product names and locations, as well as fictional names for you as a replacement for real ones.

These reports also note possible defamatory references in dialogue and actions as well as references to copyrighted material of all kinds, including clips, still photographs, books or works of art and props.

THE COPYRIGHT & TITLE SEARCH REPORT

The Insurance companies will also request a copyright & title search (and if your title is one of very many) a legal opinion

This report is a result of an elaborate and complete search of prior uses of your title as well as other similar titles. Although titles cannot be copyrighted, use of a title which is indelibly linked in the public mind with a film or television program (such as "Gone with the Wind," for example) can subject you to litigation based upon the likelihood of confusion if the title is trademarked, or on passing off if it appears your title may be linked to some previous very successful film or book. The Report can also ensure that another producer is not currently producing a film or television program of the same title. This Report will enable the producer to determine whether he can safely use his title.

These reports include a search of the U.S. Copyright Office and the Library of Congress records, common law sources that provide information on motion pictures, television, videos, dramatic works, comic books, music and current trade paper references, and Federal trademark records.

THE TITLE OR LEGAL OPINION

The Title Opinion is a document generated by an attorney in which the attorney gives an opinion which based on the information in the Title Search as to whether the title of the project is safe to use.

SPECIAL THANKS TO PEOPLE WHO HELPED ME WITH THIS BOOK

Llyswen Franks

Lacey Beers

Karen Dola

And the entire Clear Group

SUZY VAUGHAN, ESQ

She has been involved with research and legal rights clearance since 1981 when she was on staff at "Entertainment Tonight." After working as a freelance clearance administrator on such television programs as "Lifestyles of the Rich and Famous, " "Foul-ups, Bleeps & Blunders," and "The Stuntman Awards, she founded her own company in 1988 and has been assisting producers with research and clearance of clips, talent and music ever since. She has worked on programs for Michael Jackson, Barbra Streisand and Motown as well as Robin Williams and Comedy Central

For the last 10 years, she has also specialized in Copyright & Title Searches & Legal Opinions as well as Script Clearance Reports and Art Department Clearances.

She received a J.D. degree from Loyola Law School and also has a solo practice law firm, specializing in entertainment, intellectual property and music law. She wrote a paper for the Entertainment Law Journal at Loyola on fair use. She received an M.A. in English Literature from San Jose State University, an M.A. in theatre from Stanford University, a B.A. in Theatre from the University of Texas at El Paso and a certificate from the UCLA Professional Screenwriting Program. She has written a novel entitled "Hollywood Kisses," (available on Amazon). Her firm has a staff of 5, whose expertise is valuable to producers of many kinds of projects.

www.ingramcontent.com/pod-product-compliance
Lightning Source LLC
Chambersburg PA
CBHW020957180526
45163CB00006B/2399